Giraffes

Patricia Kendell

Hodder
Wayland

An imprint of Hodder Children's Books

Alligators   Chimpanzees   Dolphins   Elephants
Giraffes   Gorillas   Grizzly Bears   Hippos
Leopards   Lions   Orangutans   Pandas   Penguins
Polar Bears   Rhinos   Sea Otters   Sharks   Tigers

 © 2003 White-Thomson Publishing Ltd

Produced for Hodder Wayland by White-Thomson Publishing Ltd

Editor: Kay Barnham
Designer: Tim Mayer
Consultants: Dorcas MacClintock – Curatorial Affiliate at the
   Peabody Museum of Natural History, Yale University, USA. With
   thanks to Dr Patricia Moehlman.
Language Consultant: Norah Granger – Senior Lecturer in Primary
   Education at the University of Brighton
Picture research: Shelley Noronha – Glass Onion Pictures

Published in Great Britain in 2003 by Hodder Wayland,
an imprint of Hodder Children's Books.

Photograph acknowledgements:
Bruce Coleman 5 (Luiz Claudio Marigo); FLPA 28 (Peter Davey),
27 (David Hosking), 18 & 32 (Fritz Polking); NHPA 25 (Martin
Harvey), 26 (Jonathan & Angela Scott), cover & 10 (John Shaw);
OSF 12 (Daniel Cox), 17 (Frances Furlong), 4 (Johnny Johnson),
7 (Stan Osolinski), 20 (Richard Packwood), 8 (Mike Powles),
21 (Philip Sharp), 15 (Steve Turner); SPL 23 (John Beatty),
11 (Tim Davis), 13 (William Ervin), 9, 14 (John Reader); Still
Pictures 22 (Michel Denis-Huot), 24 (M & C Denis-Huot),
6 (Nicolas Granier), 16 (Giles Nicolet), 1 & 19 (Martin Wendler).

British Library Cataloguing in Publication Data
Kendell, Patricia
   Giraffes. – (In the wild)
   1. Giraffes – Juvenile literature
   I. Title II. Barnham, Kay
   599.6'38

ISBN: 0 7502 4225 6

Printed and bound in Hong kong

Hodder Children's Books
A division of Hodder Headline Limited
338 Euston Road, London NW1 3BH

Produced in association with WWF-UK.
WWF-UK registered charity number 1081247.
A company limited by guarantee number 4016725.
Panda device © 1986 WWF ® WWF registered trademark owner.

Contents

Where giraffes live   4

Baby giraffes   6

Looking after the calf   8

Growing up   10

Family life   12

Eating   14

Drinking   16

A giraffe's day   18

On the move   20

Resting   22

Keeping safe   24

Threats   26

Helping giraffes to survive   28

Further information   30

Glossary   31

Index   32

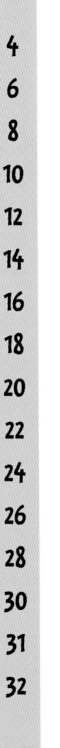

Where giraffes live

Giraffes live in Africa, in grassy places with trees and bushes.

All giraffes have patterns on their fur. No two giraffes have exactly the same pattern.

Baby giraffes

One baby, called a calf, is born a little way from the rest of the **herd**. It can stand up on its wobbly legs only an hour after it is born.

The calf soon begins to drink rich,
creamy milk from its mother.

Looking after the calf

Giraffe calves are in great danger from animals such as lions or this **hyena**. A mother will try to keep her calf well hidden in the grass.

Mothers and calves spend much time together. Mothers will also look after other calves, while their mothers look for food.

Growing up

Young calves play together. They race
and frisk around and play-fight.

They learn from their mothers where to find food and how to eat it. Male calves leave their mothers when they are about three years old.

Family life

Giraffes like being together in a herd, although they will often wander off on their own to find food.

Giraffes like to keep in touch with the herd.
They are tall enough to see over trees. Their
eyesight is so good that they can spot each
other even when they are far apart.

Eating

A giraffe's long neck allows it to reach high
up a tree for leaves, flowers and shoots.
A male can reach almost as high as six metres.

14

They **pluck** a branch with their long tongues, and strip off the leaves using their lower, comb-like teeth. They can even chew thorny twigs safely.

Drinking

When a giraffe finds a waterhole, it has to spread its front legs out, or bend its legs to drink the water.

Giraffes can go for a long time without drinking
because there is a lot of liquid in the food they eat.

A giraffe's day

A giraffe will spend between 16 and 20 hours a day eating. They sometimes eat late into the night.

After swallowing
food, the giraffe
spends a long time
chewing it up,
rather like cows do.

19

On the move

Giraffes usually walk slowly, stopping to **browse** on tasty trees as they go.

If they sense danger, then they can gallop away
at up to 56 kilometres an hour – faster than a lion.

Resting

Giraffes sometimes lie down to sleep for a short while, but getting up is quite awkward for them.

They usually rest standing up, listening for
sounds and looking out for any danger.

Keeping safe

Giraffes can see, hear
and smell very well.
They are always on
the watch for enemies.

They will use their heavy **hooves** to kick
any lion that dares to come too near.

Threats

In some parts of Africa, **poachers** catch giraffes, and kill them for their skin and meat.

The poachers make bracelets from the giraffe's tail hairs. They sell these bracelets to tourists.

Helping giraffes to survive

If tourists stop buying giraffe-hair bracelets, then poachers will not need to kill giraffes. This tourist is watching giraffes in their **home territory**.

It is important that people look after the places where giraffes live, so that these amazing animals have all the space and food that they need.

Further information

Find out more about how we can help giraffes in the future.

ORGANIZATIONS TO CONTACT

WWF-UK
Panda House, Weyside Park,
Godalming, Surrey GU7 1XR
Tel: 01483 426444
http://www.wwf.org.uk

Care for the Wild International
1 Ashfolds, Horsham Road, Rusper,
West Sussex RH12 4QX
Tel: 01293 871596
http://www.careforthewild.org.uk

BOOKS

Long-necked and leggy. Who am I?:
Moira Butterfield, Belitha Press 1998.

Giraffes (Crabapples): Bobbie Kalman,
Crabtree Publishing 1997.

The Giraffe (Animal Close-ups):
Christine Denis-Huot, Charlesbridge
Publishing 1993.

Giraffes: Long-Necked Leaf-Eaters
(Wild World of Animals): Lola M Schaefer,
Capstone Press 2001.

Glossary

WEBSITES

Most young children will need adult help when visiting websites. Those listed have child-friendly pages to bookmark.

www.nature-wildlife.com/mammals.htm
There are some good photos on this site with simple captions.

www.thebigzoo.com/Animals/Reticulated_ Giraffe.asp
This site has information and video sequences about giraffes, showing how they walk and how they use their tongues.

browse – to eat leaves and shoots from trees and bushes.

herd – a group of animals.

home territory – a place where an animal lives.

hooves – feet covered with hard horn.

hyena – a dog-like animal.

pluck – to pick.

poachers – people who hunt and kill animals without permission.

Index

B
branch 15

C
calf 6, 7, 8, 9, 10, 11

D
drink 7, 16, 17

E
eat 11, 14, 17, 18
eyesight 13

F
food 9, 11, 12, 17, 19, 29
fur 5

G
gallop 21

H
herd 6, 12, 13
hooves 25
hyena 8

L
legs 6, 16
lion 21, 25

M
milk 7
mother 7, 8, 9, 11

N
neck 14

P
play 10

S
sleep 22

T
teeth 15
tongue 15
tourists 27, 28

W
walk 20
waterhole 16